# Gymnastics

## Great Moments, Records, and Facts

### by Teddy Borth

ABDO
GREAT SPORTS
Kids

**abdopublishing.com**

Published by Abdo Kids, a division of ABDO, PO Box 398166, Minneapolis, Minnesota 55439.

Copyright © 2015 by Abdo Consulting Group, Inc. International copyrights reserved in all countries. No part of this book may be reproduced in any form without written permission from the publisher.

Printed in the United States of America, North Mankato, Minnesota.

102014

012015

THIS BOOK CONTAINS
RECYCLED MATERIALS

Photo Credits: AP Images, Corbis, Getty Images, Shutterstock, © ID1974 / Shutterstock.com p.7

Production Contributors: Teddy Borth, Jennie Forsberg, Grace Hansen

Design Contributors: Laura Rask, Dorothy Toth

Library of Congress Control Number: 2014943655

Cataloging-in-Publication Data

Borth, Teddy.

 Gymnastics : great moments, records, and facts / Teddy Borth.

   p. cm. -- (Great sports)

ISBN 978-1-62970-690-0 (lib. bdg.)

Includes bibliographical references and index.

1. Gymnastics--Juvenile literature.   I. Title.

796.44--dc23

                    2014943655

# Table of Contents

## Gymnastics

Exercises for boys were created in the 1800s. They came from old exercises from Greece. This would become gymnastics.

## The Gym

Gymnasts have 8 stations.

Women use 4 of them

for events. Men use 6.

They share 2 stations.

## Great Records

Nadia Comaneci shocked the world in 1976. She is the first to get a perfect score at the **Olympics**. She got 7 of them.

9

Kohei Uchimura won world titles five years in a row. He won the **all-around** from 2009 to 2013. He is the first to do this.

London 2012

Gabby Douglas made history in 2012. She won **Olympic gold** for **all-around**. She was the first black woman to do this.

13

## Scherbo Goes Gold

Vitaly Scherbo had one of

the best **Olympics** in 1992.

He won 6 out of 8 events.

He won the team **gold**.

He also won 5 solo events.

Only two swimmers have

won more in one **Olympics**.

## Strug Sticks the Landing

Team USA is fighting for gold in 1996. The last event is the vault. Kerri Strug is America's last hope. She falls on her first go. She hurts her ankle.

19

She must go again. She limps to the start. She runs. She lands. She scores a 9.712! USA wins its first **gold** in team gymnastics! Strug has to be carried to the medal stand.

# More Facts

- Gymnastics became an **Olympic** event in 1896. Germany won more than half of the medals.

- Artistic is the best known gymnastics type. It uses bars and beams. Other types use trampolines, hoops, or rings.

- Gymnastics looked different thousands of years ago. People used bulls. They would run toward the bull, grab the horns and jump over. They would try to land on the other side on their feet. This became a game. It was also a way to train soldiers.

# Glossary

**all-around** – an event in gymnastics that is made up of all the other events.

**gold** – given to the winner of an event.

**Olympics** – a sports event where teams and people around the world play each other. Summer games are held every four years.

# Index

## abdokids.com

Use this code to log on to abdokids.com and access crafts, games, videos, and more!

Abdo Kids Code:
GGK6900